Kate Loves Dogs

Kate Loves Dogs

By Beth Lyons

Illustrated by Natalie Marino

Xulon Elite

Xulon Press Elite
2301 Lucien Way #415
Maitland, FL 32751
407.339.4217
www.xulonpress.com

© 2017 by Beth Lyons Illustrated by Natalie Marino

All rights reserved solely by the author. The author guarantees all contents are original and do not infringe upon the legal rights of any other person or work. No part of this book may be reproduced in any form without the permission of the author. The views expressed in this book are not necessarily those of the publisher.

Unless otherwise indicated, Scripture quotations taken from the New English Translation (NET Bible). Copyright ©1996-2006 by Biblical Studies Press, L.L.C. Used by permission. All rights reserved.

Printed in the United States of America.

Edited by Xulon Press

ISBN-13: 9781545611913

For Louie and Big Dog

and all the dogs that have ever been born

and the people who love them

and God, who created us all!

A long time ago before the world was here, God was here.

God thought about you and God made plans for you — good plans.

God made plans for your heart and the things you would love.

And He still is.

God wrote His plans down in heaven.

This is a story about a little girl God thought about and made plans for.

Her name is Kate,

and Kate loves dogs.

God made plans for Kate to have dogs to love.

Real ones...and lots and lots of stuffed ones.

Kate loves her real dogs with hearts that beat,

noses that are wet, and tails that wag.

Kate loves her stuffed dogs too.

She pretends they have hearts that beat,

noses that are wet, and tails that wag.

Just like the dogs she loves, Kate has a heart that beats.

Just like the dogs she loves, Kate has a nose that is wet—

not all the time, but sometimes...

like when she eats ice cream or has a cold.

But Kate doesn't have a tail that wags.

Kate has feet that wiggle. God made her that way.

Kate wiggles her feet.

Her dogs wag their tails.

And together, they dance and dance and dance!

God kept watching Kate day after day.

He enjoys watching her play and dance with all the dogs she loves.

God kept watching Kate night after night.

One of God's favorite things to do is to watch Kate while she sleeps.

Kate dreams about her dogs, and God dreams about Kate.

He dreams about her heart and His plans for her.

One night as He watched Kate sleep, God made an important plan.

He wrote His plan down in heaven, and He wrote it on Kate's heart.

This is what God wrote:

"Dear Kate,

I love watching you love your dogs.

You will discover how much your dogs love you too.

They will show you what I am like and how much I love you."

Then God wrote...

"I love to play in the sun and dance in rain puddles.

I love to give hugs and get hugs.

I love to kiss faces — smiling happy faces

and especially faces with

tears on them.

Dogs are good at that, and so am I."

When Kate woke up the next day, her feet still wiggled as she danced with her dogs.

Her nose wasn't wet. Yet something was new.

Her heart felt bigger and beat louder than before.
It felt full of plans and hopes and lots of dreams.
It even felt like God was dancing there.

Kate knew something important had happened.
And she knew God wanted to dance inside all the hearts all over the world.

Every day and every night, God is still thinking about Kate,

and God is still thinking about you.

God is making plans for Kate,

and God is making plans for you — good plans.

God is making plans for Kate's heart and for your heart and

the things you love.

God is writing His plans down in heaven.

He is writing them on Kate's heart and on your heart,

sometimes as you both are sleeping...

so you and Kate

can invite the rest of the world

to dance with God, too!

Afterward to Kate Loves Dogs

Having used the scripture reference in Jeremiah 29:11 for this story, I decided some months later to review again the context and setting of this Old Testament book. God led me to explore Jeremiah 31. This entire chapter is a beautiful picture of restoration. Here I highlight only Jeremiah 31:33 which says, "But this is the covenant which I will make with the house of Israel after those days," declares the Lord. "I will put My law within them, and on their heart I will write it; and I will be their God, and they shall be My people." (NAS Bible). I was blessed by this discovery and once again entrusted the publishing of Kate Loves Dogs to Him.

Dear friends, may your hearts be restored to the God who made you and loves you. Your life is a grand story being written in heaven and within you. Let Him revive your hopes and dreams if perhaps you have forgotten them. Be you, for there is only one. And may you find yourself being awakened to the presence of God dancing in your heart.

www.ingramcontent.com/pod-product-compliance
Lightning Source LLC
LaVergne TN
LVHW060133080526
838201LV00118B/3043